The Mystery of the Giant Claw

The Mystery of the Giant Claw

Written by Katie Parsons
& The HedgeHunter Team
Illustrated by Poppie Andrew

First Published in 2022 by Fantastic Books Publishing
Cover illustration by Poppie Andrew
Cover design by Gabi

With the support of the University of Hull
ISBN (hardback): 978-1-914060-40-3
ISBN (paperback): 978-1-914060-41-0
ISBN (ebook): 978-1-914060-42-7

HedgeHunter Team

Lucie
Poppie
Saskia
Lisa
Katie

Summer

Oliver

Kit

Josh

James

James
Kit
Oliver
Summer
Josh

Dedication

We dedicate this book to all the young environmental activists out there around the world, trying to protect the planet. These people give up their free time trying to engage others in what is happening and making changes within their communities, whether it's taking action to organise a local litter pick or standing up and addressing policymakers in parliament. You are all amazing and together we can make the changes that are needed for our future.

Acknowledgements

We would like to thank the Ernest Cook Trust for funding this work as part of their Green Influencers Scheme. East Riding Voluntary Action Service (ERVAS) and their Volunteen section have been instrumental in supporting our ideas – with a specific thank you to Lisa Harris.

Additionally, we would like to thank the Ferens Education Trust at the University of Hull for funding the start of our journey.

A special thank you however goes to Fred and Nicky Wood, who are the real farmers and owners of Little Wood Farm in the East Riding of Yorkshire. They have allowed the team to use their land for experiments and surveying of hedgerows to help inform this project, helping to inform and educate young people. The whole team is forever grateful.

Once upon a time there was a small brown prickly little hedgehog called Hunter.

Hunter lived in a hedgerow in the village of Little Primrose and loved her home very much.

One day Hunter decided to go for a walk, as it was beautiful sunny weather.

On her journey, as Hunter walked past a field of sheep, she heard a small muffled voice coming from a nearby pile of leaves.

'Help me,' it said.

'Who said that?' Hunter felt a little scared as she could not see who was talking.

'It's me,' said the little voice, and just at that moment Hunter saw a small thin hand emerge from the leaves.

Hunter pulled at the hand and out popped a thin and prickly branch.

'I'm Twig …' said the branch as he dusted off the leaves from the top of his head. 'Thank you for helping me.'

'But what were you doing there?' asked Hunter.

So Twig told Hunter the story of how he had ended up under a bed of leaves.

'I was sitting in my hedge reading my favourite book and eating some berries … Oh! A berry …' Twig grabbed one from the floor and went on, '… when a big sharp red claw came roaring towards me. Next thing I knew I was stuck under the leaves and on the floor.'

Twig looked up at his house, with his mouth full. He began to cry.

'My house …' he sobbed. 'My beautiful house.'

Poor Twig's house had been ruined. All that was left was half of his chair and a squashed red berry.

To cheer Twig up, Hunter said, 'Let's go together and find out what did this to your house. I have lots of friends here in Little Primrose that I am sure can help us out … That's if you would like to be my friend?'

Twig smiled. 'Oh yes, please, I would love to be your friend. I don't have many friends. I get called names due to being twiggy and prickly.'

Twig looked at the floor, all sad again.

'Don't worry, Twig. Look, I'm prickly too, due to my spikes. I use them to defend myself against predators. They are like a superpower.'

Twig liked this. 'Wow, I never thought of it like that. Just call me Super Twig.'

Hunter laughed and the pair walked on hand-in-hand down Hedgerow Lane.

On their journey they bumped into Dorothy the dormouse and her three mischievous children Daisy, Douglas and Dale.

Dorothy was laden with bags full of disused plastic bottles and wrappers.

Out of the corner of Hunter's eye she saw the cheeky children looking into some silver foil from a disused crisp packet, pulling funny faces at each other. Twig ran over to join in.

Confused, Hunter said, 'Hello Dorothy, what have you got there?'

Dorothy explained that she could not find any leaves this year to make her home all cosy for her children. 'But I've found lots and lots of plastic so I'll have to use that.'

Dorothy went on, 'A big, sharp red claw came out of nowhere and took all the leaves away.'

Twig stopped pulling faces and shouted, 'Which way did it go?'

Dorothy pointed down the path.

Hunter and Twig thanked her and hurried in the direction Dorothy had pointed.

Hunter was very sad. She knew that plastic was bad for animals. She was more determined than ever to find out what this big sharp red claw was.

Further along the lane they saw Samaria the red squirrel.

Samaria had a bandage around her arm and a cut just above her eye.

'What on earth happened to you, Samaria? Are you ok?' said a concerned Hunter, who was taken aback at seeing her in such a state.

'Yes, I am alright now,' said Samaria with a tear in her eye. 'But as I was collecting berries yesterday, a big sharp silver claw came over from nowhere and cut all my berries away and did this to me.' Samaria pointed to her arm then burst into tears.

'My beautiful big juicy berries,' she sobbed.

'What on earth is happening, Twig?'
asked Hunter after they had left
Samaria.

'I have never seen my friends so
upset. Poor Samaria, and hers wasn't
a red claw like yours and Dorothy's
but a silver one. And she wasn't on
Hedgerow Lane but in the Jones' back
garden. This is becoming a mystery.'

'I think we might need some help.'

At that very moment a gust of wind rustled through Hedgerow Lane and flapped the edges of a big colourful poster pinned to a fence.

'Look,' said Twig. 'I think these are the people who can help us.'

The poster had big smiling faces on it and read:

We are the HedgeHunters. Here to protect hedgerows and all species that live in them.

Hunter and Twig called up the number from the poster and told the HedgeHunters all about their problem.

'Yes, it was a big sharp red claw and then turned into a big sharp silver claw … on Hedgerow Lane and then spotted in the Jones' back garden!'

The HedgeHunters said they thought they knew what it might be and agreed to meet Twig and Hunter at Little Wood Farm in 20 minutes.

When Hunter and Twig arrived at Little Wood Farm, the HedgeHunters were already waiting for them.

They shook hands with Lucie, Saskia and James. Then Kit, Summer, Oliver and Poppie stepped forward to say hello

'Hi, it's great to meet you both,' said Lucie.

'I'm glad you came,' beamed Saskia.

James began to tell Hunter and Twig that they had been receiving lots of phone calls lately and had been investigating the problem.

'We think we have found out what's been happening,' said Kit.

Just at that moment the ground began to move. A roaring noise thundered through the air. Twig and Hunter began to shake.

'Don't worry,' said Summer, 'we will look after you.'

As the noise grew louder, a bright red tractor came round the corner. Attached to the tractor was a giant hedge cutter. It roared towards them.

'It's the bright red claw!' shouted Twig.

'STOP!!!!' yelled Oliver, waving at the tractor to halt.

He raced over to the tractor. The farmer climbed out, looking shocked.

'You need to stop cutting all of the hedges. It's not the right time! It's home to so many animals and plants, and they are getting hurt!'

The farmer looked very sad.

'I'm really sorry, everyone, I didn't realise anybody was getting hurt. I just thought I was doing the right thing. How can I make things right?'

'Hmm …' Twig thought for a moment. 'I know! How about you help us to teach everyone when they should cut hedgerows and how good they are for the environment.'

'OK,' said the farmer. 'I would very much like to help do that.' He pulled out a big bag of juicy berries and gave them to Hunter and Twig.

'Mmm …' Twig licked his lips. Soon there was juice dripping down his face. 'These are delic–'

Suddenly they heard the roaring of another engine. Hunter once again began to quiver in fear.

'Oh no, not again!' he cried.

'What is that?' asked James.

'That,' said Saskia angrily, 'must be the silver claw that Samaria the squirrel was talking about.'

They all raced over to see what was causing such a noise and found Mrs Jones standing on top of a ladder. In her hand was the big silver claw, with moving giant teeth.

'STOP!!!!' they all shouted at once.

Kit and Oliver began to tell her about the dangers of cutting hedgerows at the wrong time of the year and how she had been harming the animals.

Mrs Jones looked upset and told them she felt awful, because the last thing she wanted to do was to hurt the animals.

'I'm so very sorry,' she said. 'If you tell me when, I will promise only to cut back my hedges at those times.'

Mrs Jones made a pot of elderflower tea and some spiced berry cakes for Twig after he had eyed some on her kitchen worktop.

'Mmmm …' he said with crumbs falling to the floor and a mouthful of cake. 'Do you have any more?'

They spent the rest of the afternoon sitting in the sun coming up with ideas for how they could protect hedgerows and the species that lived in them.

'Great', said Summer enthusiastically when they had settled on a plan. 'This should do it.'

'See what you can achieve when you work together,' said Lucie as she giggled at Twig biting into his fourth slice of cake.

The next day they rounded up the villagers of Little Primrose and invited them to a Hedgerows Celebration Day at the village hall.

They had put up posters all about looking after hedgerows and the wildlife in them.

Mrs Jones had made more of her berry cake, much to Twig's delight, and showed the villagers which hedgerows to pick the berries from.

As the day finished and the villagers went home, Hunter and Twig thanked the HedgeHunters for all their help.

Kit asked if they would like to become honorary members of the HedgeHunters to which Hunter and Twig shouted a big, 'YES!!'

Saskia must have hoped they would say this because she had made them special badges and caps, which she presented to them.

'Thank you so much,' they both said.

'Does this mean we are all friends?' said Twig.

'Of course,' said Oliver. 'We will be best friends forever.'

'But for now,' said James excitedly, 'let's party!'

Relaxed and relieved, the animals of Little Primrose all came out of their hiding places, feeling confident that the HedgeHunters would help to keep them safe and secure.

'Look at me,' shouted Twig as he danced a jig on the farmer's tractor.

They giggled at his prickly little feet tapping away and knew that today they were all happy and safe together.

The End

About the HedgeHunter Team

The HedgeHunter project was born when researchers Katie Parsons and Josh Wolstenholme from the University of Hull were looking to engage young people in their work exploring the importance of hedgerows and gaps in hedgerows across the East Riding of Yorkshire. You can stay up to speed with our work, including tips on what sorts of creatures live in hedgerows and when is best to cut them, through our zine which is available on our project website tinyurl.com/hedgehunters

James

Hi, I'm James. I love science and the sea.

Kit

Hi, I'm Kit. I love to learn new things and explore new places. The HedgeHunter project is an amazing way for me to meet new people and do new things, as well as connect with nature.

Lucie

Hi, I'm Lucie. I'm an environmental activist and ambassador for several environmental focused projects and I love exploring the outdoors. Reading is another one of my passions, as well as being creative and being a scout.

Oliver

Hi, I'm Oliver and I love to play football and I like to read action-adventure books. My favourite food is lasagne, I love spending time outdoors and going on adventures with Scouts.

Poppie

Hi, I'm Poppie and I love being part of the HedgeHunter team because I love looking after our hedges and the wildlife that lives in them.

Saskia

Hi! I'm Saskia. I love animals, wildlife and nature as well as reading, writing and art. I am also creating a wildflower meadow in our village.

Summer

Hi, I'm Summer and I am a HedgeHunter. I love doing wildlife photography and educational videos. I love hedgehogs, seals and foxes.

Katie Parsons

Hi, I'm Katie and I am a researcher and a youth worker. I work with children and young people on environmental and climate change projects.

Josh Wolstenholme

Hi, I'm Josh and I am a researcher in energy and the environment. I lead the wider 'Hedgerows: Mapping the Gaps' project.

Lisa Harris

Hi, I'm Lisa and I am a youth worker in the East Riding of Yorkshire supporting young people with environmental social action.

The Ernest Cook Trust

The Ernest Cook Trust is one the UK's leading educational charities. We provide funding to schools and youth groups to increase learning from the land and delivery directly to groups on our own sites.

Since 2020, we have been funding the Green Influencers Scheme with match-funding from the #iwill fund. The #iwill Fund supports the aims of the #iwill movement - to make involvement in social action a part of life for young people, by recognising the benefit for both young people and their communities.

The #iwill Fund is made possible thanks to £66 million joint investment from The National Lottery Community Fund and the Department for Digital, Culture, Media and Sport (DCMS) to support young people to access high quality social action opportunities. The Ernest Cook Trust is acting as a match funder and awarding grants on behalf of the #iwill Fund.

www.ernestcooktrust.org.uk

Proudly supporting
youth social action

#iwill

Green Influencers Scheme

The Green Influencers Scheme brings together 36 youth and environment organisations across England and funds a Green Mentor post at each organization. Green Mentors work with groups of Green Influencers to learn about climate and environmental issues and identify ways to tackle these for the benefit of their local communities.

Please get in touch with us at greeninfluencers@ernestcooktrust.org.uk for more information on environmental youth social action and how to get involved.

Volunteen at ERVAS has had the privilege of being one of the 36 organisations funded for the Green Influencers Scheme. The HedgeHunters are one of the groups we have had the pleasure of supporting on this wider project. We are incredibly proud of this work along with other youth projects across the East Riding of Yorkshire. If you would like to hear more about Volunteen please visit contact office@ervas.org.uk.

EAST RIDING VOLUNTARY ACTION SERVICES (ERVAS) LTD
"The Charity for Charities and Communities"

Tell us about your own hedgerow adventures in these notes pages

Notes

Notes

Notes

Notes

Notes

Notes

Notes

Notes

Notes

If you have enjoyed this book, please consider leaving a review for the HedgeHunter Team on Goodreads or Amazon to let them know what you thought of their work.

You can read more about the HedgeHunter Team
and their work at
tinyurl.com/hedgehunters

If you would like to find out more about their work follow
@parsnipsparsons @josh_nfm
@TheHedgeHunters on twitter

www.fantasticbooksstore.com

www.ingramcontent.com/pod-product-compliance
Lightning Source LLC
Chambersburg PA
CBHW070758050426
42452CB00012B/2389